STARTING GEOGRAPHY

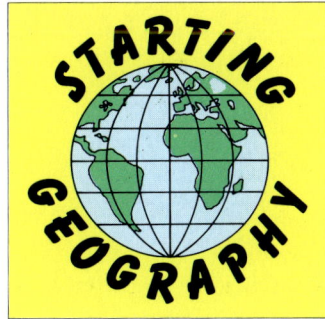

Conservation

Written by
Nigel Nelson

Illustrated by
Robert Wheeler

Wayland

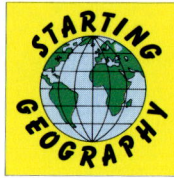

Books in the series

Clothes and Costumes   Landscapes
Conservation   Resources
Houses and Homes   Water
Journeys   Weather and Climate

First published in 1992 by
Wayland (Publishers) Ltd
61 Western Road, Hove
East Sussex, BN3 1JD. England

Series editor: Mandy Suhr
Designer: Jean Wheeler

British Library Cataloguing in Publication Data

Nelson, Nigel
Conservation.–(Starting Geography Series)
I. Title   II. Series
333.7

HARDBACK ISBN 0-7502-0458-3

PAPERBACK ISBN 0-7502-0800-7

Typeset by Dorchester Typesetting Group Ltd
Printed in Italy by Rotolito Lombarda, S.p.A., Milan
Bound in France by A.G.M.

Contents

The words in **bold** are explained in the glossary.

What is conservation?

At one time there were not many people on Earth. The things in nature which were needed for food, shelter or **fuel**, (our resources) could be used without really changing the world.

But the number of people on Earth is growing. Many of our **natural resources** will run out unless we begin to use less of them, or find other things to use instead.

In nature there is no waste. Everything is broken down and used again. But people do make waste and this can **pollute** the **environment**.

Conservation means finding ways
to look after our planet, and all
our resources, more carefully.

Plant and animal homes

The natural home of a group of plants and animals, like a pond or field, is called a habitat.

As more houses, factories and roads are built for people, many habitats are destroyed. Without a home to live in or food to eat, many plants and animals may die. ▼

Pollution can also destroy habitats. Chemicals and waste poured into the environment can kill the plants and animals that have made their homes there.

Litter can be very dangerous to animals and birds. This weasel has become trapped in an old bottle.

Conserve a habitat

Is there a piece of waste ground or a pond near you that could be cleared of litter and junk? Tell your parents about it and ask them to help you.

You can buy packets of wildflower seeds to plant.

8

You might even help to dig your own pond. All sorts of plants and creatures will make their home there. You will provide a new habitat for creatures like dragon-flies, butterflies, frogs, newts and hedgehogs.

Activity

Attract birds to your garden! You can feed them in the winter with peanuts, coconut, crumbs and scraps. Make a peanut-feeder out of old milk cartons or yoghurt pots.

Save our trees!

Trees are very important to life on Earth. From them we get food, **timber**, medicines and other useful things. They also provide habitats for all sorts of creatures.

Trees help to make the air good to breathe. In the past, great forests covered the Earth and nobody ever thought that we would run out of trees.

Today, many new trees have to be planted to make up for the ones that have been cut down.

Activity

Grow your own trees:
1. Collect the seeds from different trees.

2. Put some soil in flower pots and plant one seed near to the top in each pot. Water it, to keep the soil damp.

3. When the **seedling** is about 10 cm high, take it out of the pot and plant it.

11

The tropical rainforests

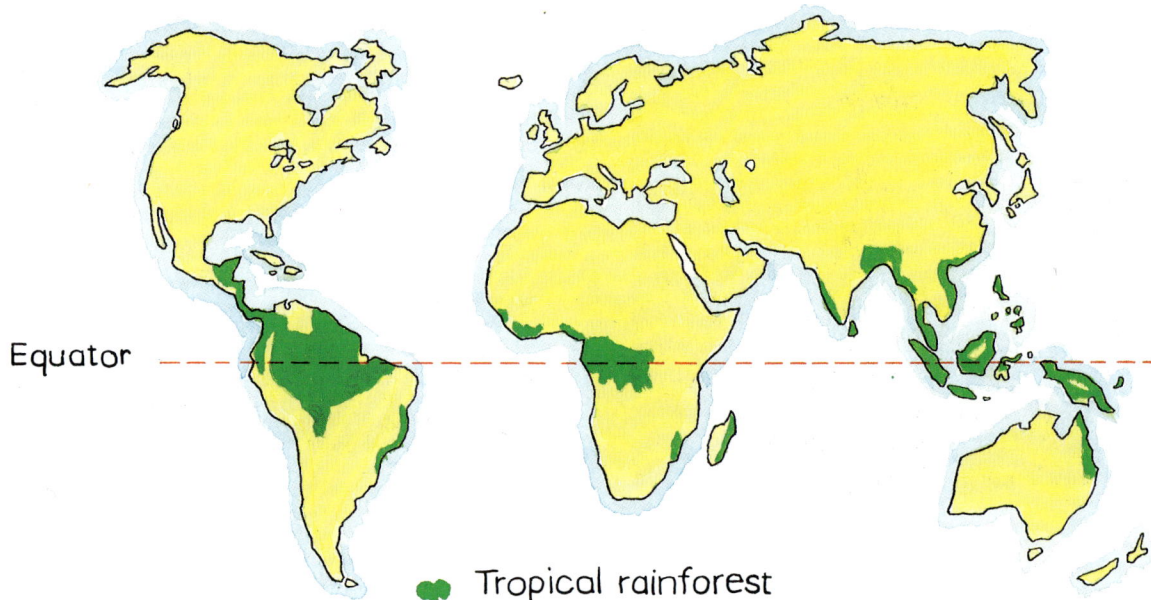

Equator

Tropical rainforest

Tropical rainforests are found in the lands around the **Equator** where it is always hot and wet. An amazing number of plants, birds, insects, fish and other animals live there.

The people who have lived in the forest for thousands of years do no harm to the forest. Now, many of them are losing their homes and wildlife is being destroyed for ever. This is because the trees in the rainforest are being cut down for their valuable wood.

These children live in the rainforests of Panama.

The forest is being burned
down to make way for crops,
or land, on which to graze
cows for beef.

But the rainforests are too
important to lose. They
affect the world's **climate**
and probably contain
many new medicines and foods.
People have started to try
and stop the destruction
of the rainforests.

Animals in danger

There are animals and birds in danger in all countries of the world. Some creatures are now extinct, which means that there are none left on the Earth at all.

The Dodo bird used to live on Earth, but it was hunted until there were none left. ▶

Some creatures like leopards, pandas and whales are in danger of becoming extinct. ▼

Some rare animals are still being hunted, even when it is against the law. African elephants are hunted and killed for their ivory tusks. ▲

Other rare and beautiful animals are killed for their skins or fur to make expensive coats and bags. ▶

Laws protecting wild animals are often broken. But many people all over the world are working hard to conserve wildlife.

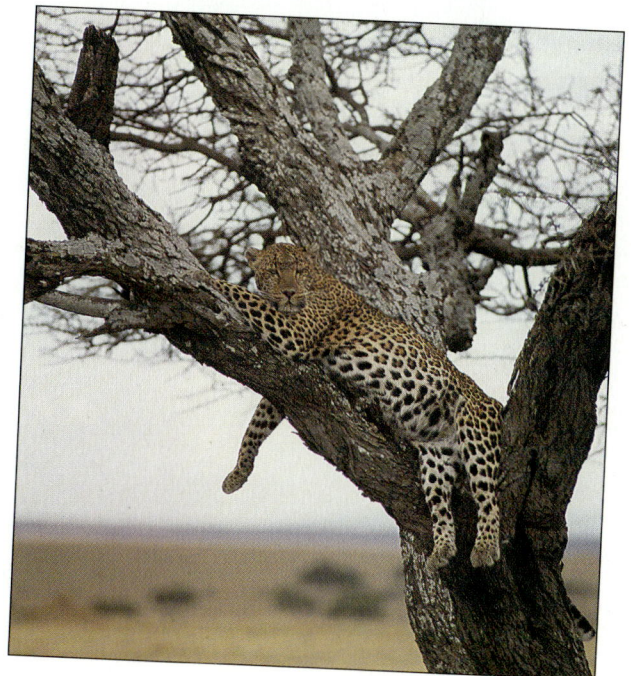

15

National parks and game reserves

◄ People around the world have joined conservation groups to help wildlife. Not everybody likes to see wild animals kept in zoos, but some zoos help to keep rare animals from becoming extinct, like this panda.

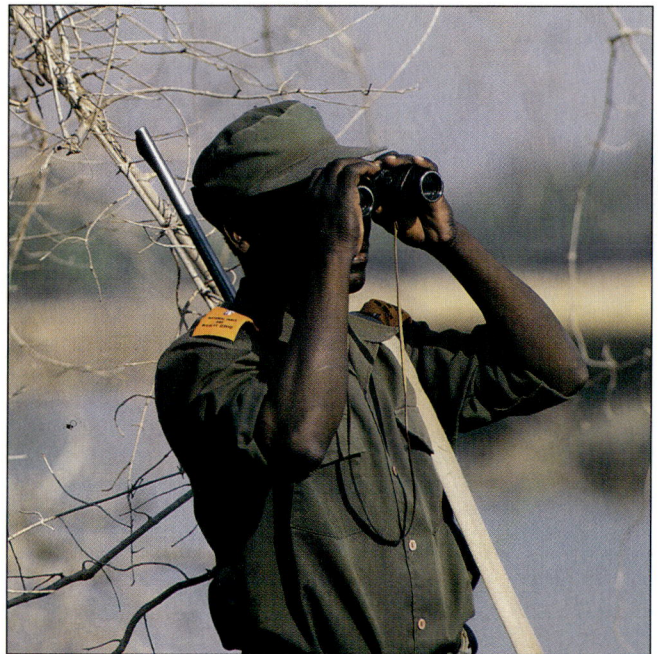

▲ National parks and **game reserves** have been set up where birds and animals can live in peace in their own habitats. This **game warden** works in a game reserve in Zambia. He is watching for ivory **poachers**.

If reserves, like this one, had not been set up to protect the North American bison, there would be none alive today. ▲

Activity

Write a letter to one of the conservation groups listed at the back of the book and ask for more information. Many of them have special information packs for children.

A load of rubbish

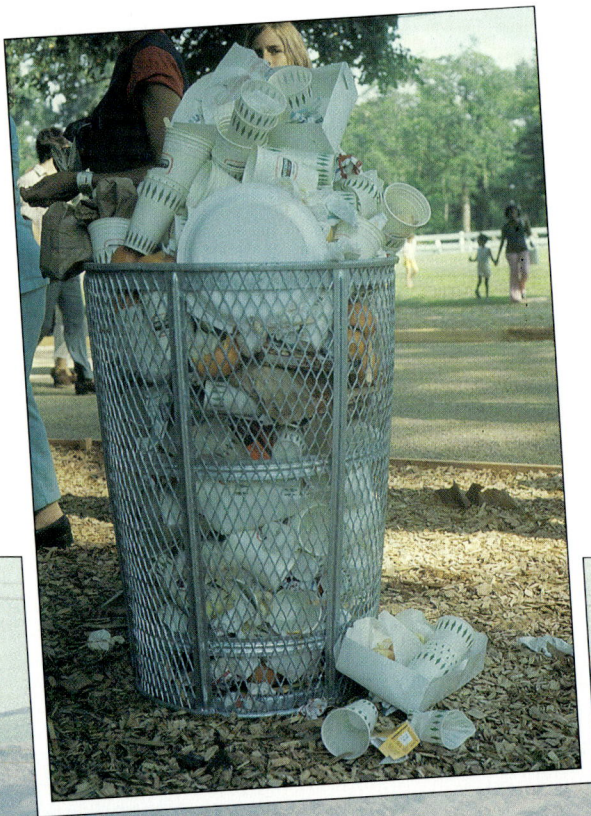

Unlike nature, people produce large amounts of rubbish. Waste which harms the land, water or air is called pollution.

Most of the rubbish from our homes gets taken away by trucks and buried under the ground. Some of this rots away but materials such as plastic, stay in the ground and will never rot. ▼

Waste and dirty water from our sinks and toilets pass through sewers to **sewage farms** where the water is cleaned.

Sometimes sewage and waste chemicals are dumped straight into the sea, killing sea-life and making it dangerous to swim. ▲

Activity

Which rubbish rots?
1. With an adult, bury different types of rubbish in the ground and mark with sticks where they are.
2. Dig them up again after a month. Which things have rotted?

Fighting pollution

We can all fight pollution. You can help to clear litter and you should never drop it.

Car fumes can pollute the air and harm the people who breathe them. A metal called lead can be found in some petrol. This is poisonous. Many people are now changing over to cars that have cleaner fumes because they run on lead-free petrol. ▶

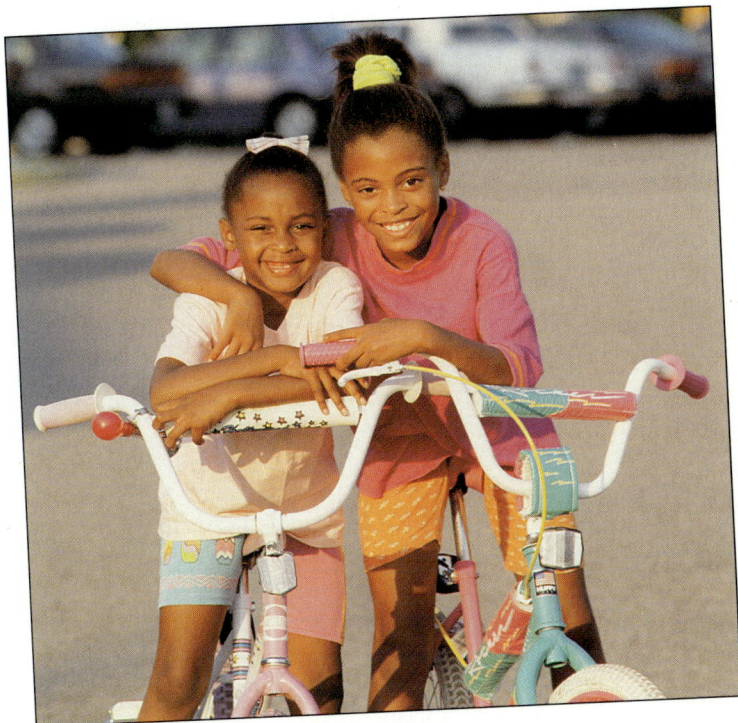

▲ There would be less pollution from traffic if we used **public transport** more, like these trams in Hong Kong. Walking and cycling also help stop pollution.

Scientists have found that the gases in some **aerosols** can harm part of the **atmosphere** called the **ozone layer**. Because of this, many people have decided not to use them.

Recycling

Throwing things away is a waste of our resources. It makes more sense to change our rubbish into things we can use again. This is called recycling.

Rubbish can be sorted out into glass, paper, and cans. These can be taken to a recycling centre. If you have a garden, natural waste, like orange peel or egg shells, can be used to make **compost** which is very good for the soil.

Recycling also saves **energy**. It takes much less energy to recycle things like bottles and cans than it takes to make completely new ones.

These cans are being melted down to use again.

All these things have been made from recycled paper. What other products can you find that have been recycled?

Activity

Make your own recycled paper.

1. Tear up newspaper into small pieces and soak them in water overnight.

2. Mash it all up with a fork.

3. Drain out the water, roll out the mixture with a rolling pin and let it dry.

Fossil fuels

Oil, gas, and coal are called fossil fuels because they are made from the remains of animals and plants that died millions of years ago.

Most electricity is made in **power stations**, like this one, that burn fossil fuels.

The gases given off by power stations can cause acid rain. This happens when the gases mix with rainwater and make it sour or acid. Acid rain poisons forests, lakes and rivers. ▲

◄ It also damages buildings, like this stone statue in Cracow, Poland.

Some power stations are now being changed so they make less pollution.

Power from nature

Most of the energy we use in our homes comes from fossil fuels or **nuclear power**. But fossil fuels can cause pollution and will run out in the future. Nuclear power produces harmful waste and can be very dangerous if accidents happen.

Scientists are trying to use natural resources, such as the sun, wind and water to produce energy. These don't damage the environment and will not run out. They can be used over and over again.

The energy from the sun can be used to produce **solar power**. ▼

▲ Special windmills, like these in the USA, use the wind to make electricity. The energy in falling water is also used to make electricity. This river power station is in Austria. ▼

What can you do?

It is very important that we begin to do things to conserve our Earth and its wildlife now. There are many things that we can all do.

We should recycle things whenever we can. This way we will not waste our resources. These children are collecting cans for recycling. ▲

It is easy to conserve energy just by making sure that we switch off lights and other electrical things when we are not using them. ▶

Think hard about the things you buy in shops. Choose things which do the least harm to the planet. Also, try to choose things which do not have a lot of wasteful packaging.

◄ This girl is re-using plastic cartons as plant pots. In this way she is recycling them herself!

Activity

Make a poster to tell other people about the ways in which they can look after our planet Earth.

Glossary

Aerosol A spray can.

Atmosphere The layer of air around the Earth.

Climate The pattern of weather that a place has throughout the year.

Compost A mixture of rotted waste that is added to soil which helps plants to grow.

Energy Power which makes other things work.

Environment All the things around us like the land, the air, the water, the plants and the animals.

Equator An imaginary line going round the middle of the Earth.

Fuel Anything that is burned to produce heat or power.

Game reserve A large area of land set aside for the protection of wildlife.

Game warden Someone who works on a game reserve to protect wildlife.

Natural resources All the things found in nature which are useful.

Nuclear power A useful form of power which produces waste which can be dangerous.

Ozone layer Part of the atmosphere where there is ozone gas. This protects the Earth from the Sun's harmful rays.

Poacher A person who hunts animals against the law.

Pollutes Makes dirty or harms the environment.

Pollution Anything which harms or makes dirty our air, water, or life on land.

Power station A place where electricity is produced.

Public transport Vehicles, such as trains or buses, for which people pay to be taken from place to place.

Seedling A baby tree.

Sewage farm A place where dirty water from homes and factories is cleaned.

Solar power Power created by trapping the heat of the sun.

Timber Wood that is used for building.

Finding out more

Books to Read

What can we do about litter? by Donna Bailey (Franklin Watts, 1992)

What can we do about recycling rubbish by Donna Bailey (Franklin Watts, 1992)

The Blue Peter Green Book (BBC Books, 1991)

Clean Air Dirty Air by L Parchett (A & C Black, 1990)

Where Does Rubbish Go? by S Tahta (Usborne, 1991)

Waste and Recycling by B Taylor (A & C Black, 1990)

My First Green Book by A Wilkes (Dorling Kindersley, 1991)

Useful Addresses

World Wide Fund for Nature
Panda House
Weyside Park
Catteshall Lane
Godalming, Surrey
GU7 1XR

Friends of the Earth
26-28 Underwood St
London N1 7JQ

Greenpeace
Canonbury Villas
London N1 2PN

WATCH
The Green
Witham Park
Waterside South
Lincoln
LN5 7JR

Whale and Dolphin Conservation Society
19a James Street West
Bath, Avon
BA1 2BT

Index

Picture acknowledgements
The photographs in this book were supplied by: Bruce Coleman 16 (right); Ecoscene cover, 5, 6 (below), 10, 11 (below), 13 (above and below), 18 (below), 20 (above and below), 22 (below), 23, 25 (above), 28, 29; F.L.P.A. 6 (above), 7, 15 (centre), 17, 19; Photri 18 (above), 22 (above), 27 (below); Science Photo Library 25 (below); Tony Stone Worldwide 8, 11 (above), 15 (above), 24, 26, 27 (above); Topham 15 (below); Wayland Picture Library 4 (below), 21 (above), 26 (above), 28 (below); Zefa 4, 11 (centre), 12, 14, 16 (left), 21.